Lean Enterprise

Step-by-Step Guide to Lean Enterprise

(Lean Concepts, Lean Tools, Lean Thinking, and How to
Foster Innovation and Validate New Ideas Through Lean)

I0492848

Jason Bennett & Jennifer Bowen

Table of Contents

Introduction

I want to thank you for choosing this book, 'Lean Business'

American cartoonist and author Allen Saunders once said: *"Life is what happens to you while you are busy making other plans."* Some people will have you believe that John Lennon said it, but that is not true.

Regardless of who made this statement, it highlights an enigma that can be applied to businesses too. A business must be able to adapt to change since things rarely go according to what was planned. The same can be said for teams too.

In the era of technology, most businesses are shifting towards automation and artificial intelligence. The machine can do many processes. However, there are only a few businesses that are willing to accept that change.

For instance, if you own a company that sells floppy disks, you know you will never be able to make sales because the world has moved on from floppy disks. The same can be said about processes that are worked on in organizations.

Many processes in an organization or a team become redundant over a period after which they must be removed. This is when a company becomes a lean business. Over the course of the book, you will learn about lean businesses and their principles.

You will also gather information on how lean businesses foster innovations and how those innovations are used to improve the business culture.

Every employee in an organization is asked to learn the process he or she is working on and understand why that process is being worked on.

However, the material provided for learning is often considered waste since there are multiple changes made to the processes. A lean business ensures that its employees undergo a great learning and development program, which will help them hone their skills and capabilities.

This book covers some tips that can be used to make learning lean in your organization.

Thank you for purchasing the book. I hope you gather the information you were looking for.

Chapter One: What is Lean?

The core principle of lean is to minimize waste and maximize customer value. In other words, lean is to provide customers with products and services of greater value while using fewer resources.

Every lean business understands what the customers want and focuses on improving fundamental processes to meet those demands. The goal is to provide the customer with products and services of exceptional value through a process that has minimal or zero waste.

Lean thinking will change the areas that are focused on by management to accomplish this. Instead of focusing on separate technology, vertical departments and assets, the management will focus on how the flow of products and services can be optimized horizontally across assets, technology and departments to its customers.

The management will also need to look at how waste processes can be eliminated along the value stream. It will need to look at how processes can be optimized to reduce human time, human effort, space and capital, which help to reduce the cost incurred to finish the product or service.

Such companies can respond to the changing needs of their customers with high quality, high variety, speed and low cost. Information management will also become more accurate and more straightforward.

Lean Management for Production and Services

Most people believe that lean management works best in manufacturing. This is not true. Lean management can be applied to different businesses and processes and is not a cost reduction program or a tactic. It is a way of acting and thinking for the whole organization.

Businesses in all sectors and industries, including government and healthcare have started to use the lean principle to change the way they work and think. Many organizations choose not to call this type of management lean, but state that it is their system.

You may wonder why organizations do this. It is done to drive home the fact that lean management is not a short or long-term cost reduction program but is the way the company operates.

The term lean transformation is used to define a company that is moving away from old thinking towards a new way or lean way of thinking. This means that the company has started to change the way business is conducted which takes perseverance.

The term lean was coined in the late 1980s by a James Womack, Ph.D., who was leading a research team at an International Motor Vehicle Program at MIT, to describe Toyota's business.

Lean Business Principles

Lean business principles entered the American business market in the early 1990s through the book "Lean Thinking." Lean thinking originated in the manufacturing models in Toyota automotive in the late 1980s after the introduction of Kanban. Lean models are now used in different industries to reduce time spent on delivering high-quality products and reducing the number of resources used to achieve that goal. Let us take a look at some lean model principles.

Value Identification

It is important to remember that value to a company begins and ends only with the stakeholders or customers. If a customer requires a specific product or service from your company, you must use all the resources you need to deliver the product within the stipulated time. It is essential for every business to identify the products or services that will add value to its customers.

Value Stream Mapping

When a business identifies the products and services that provide value to its customers, it should map every process and procedure that the company must follow to manufacture or produce that product or service. It is during the mapping process that the business can identify the steps that contribute to waste or add no value to the goal. For instance, if the business discovers the process to place orders by employees is complicated, it must either eliminate that process since it is a waste contributor.

Flow

When the business creates the process map, it will identify the steps that are unnecessary or waste contributors. The business must then remove those processes or steps to create a flow. This flow will ensure that there are no obstacles that will hinder the delivery of products or services to customers. For instance, if a gardening service must visit an off-site location to stock up on supplies, it will take a longer time to deliver its services. The business must look at whether it can increase on-site storage space to enhance the flow of the process.

Pull

Lean processes always produce based on the demand from customers, which makes the processes "pull processes." Pull processes are those that call for the production of products and services on an as-wanted or as-needed basis. In service businesses, the delivery is always dependent on the workforce. For example, a pizza delivery service can choose to hire delivery executives based on the demand for pizza. If it is football season, there are bound to be more orders from customers. It is prudent for the business to hire more delivery executives during that period.

Perfection

It is important for a business to continually refine the first four principles to ensure that processes have minimal or no waste in them. The idea behind this principle is that any waste that goes unnoticed in the first four stages is always exposed over time. It is important to eliminate that waste to help a business adapt to the changing needs of its customers.

Peter Hines has argued that the five principles of lean thinking may be insufficient for some or most contemporary business situations. He stated that businesses need to apply lean thinking only to some processes like order fulfillment without giving any regard to communication, leadership or quality management.

Therefore, it is essential to understand how lean thinking can be applied to help a business develop a holistic approach to the delivery of products and services.

Chapter Two: Lean Concepts and Tools

Lean companies employ the support of many concepts and tools that support the principles and also help to eliminate waste from the processes. This chapter covers some of the most critical tools that every business must be aware of.

Takt Time

A lean business must always look at ways to optimize processes to ensure that its customers and stakeholders are happy with the rate at which they have received their products. Takt time is the average rate at which any business must produce or execute products or transactions respectively based on the customer's requirements and in the stipulated time.

Takt = (Time available to produce a product or service) / (Demands made by the customer)

Cellular Manufacturing

Cellular marketing aims to reduce the time taken to meet the customer or market's demand and also to bring processes that produce similar products together. Workstations and equipment are arranged to bring different teams to manufacture similar products.

Continuous Flow

This tool ensures that the batch size is reduced to eliminate some constraints in the system. The business must identify a method by which it produces products or information that moves at a consistent pace from one step that adds value to the next with zero delays or waste in between.

Standardized Work

The business must create a document that lists out the processes or methods being used to produce goods and services to meet the calculated takt time. This helps to standardize tasks and enhance the full value stream.

Kanban and Pull Systems

Kanban is a tool used to schedule tasks and also instruct different departments with the tasks that it must complete to produce or manufacture different products and services. This tool was developed by Taiichi Ohno to improve the manufacturing process of Toyota automotive in the late 1980s. Every business must include a customer process that signals the manufacture or supply process to deliver the final product.

The Whys

A business must always ask the question "why" to get to the root of any problem that may arise during the process cycle. For example, if there is a delay to receive the raw material from the supplier, the business can ask the following questions:

- Why are we sticking to this supplier only?
- Why is there no backup supplier?

Level the Workload

Customer patterns are often variable, and the processes in every business are consistent in the sense that every process must be built to manage a defined quantity of work. This strategy can be adopted by many businesses to plan different types and volumes of work.

Problem Solving

Most companies implementing lean thinking in their business adopt the PDCA cycle, which is a logical and graphical representation of how most individuals in the company have solved problems. This allows the company to think that every process, regardless of the department, is a part of the process.

Plan: Establish the plan to achieve the final goal

Do: Implement the plan

Check: Collect, collate and analyze the results

Act: Implement reforms only if the business is unable to obtain the desired results

The business can create a system that can identify and solve problems by understanding the cause and implementing countermeasures to eliminate the problem.

Chapter Three: How to use Validated Ideas to Improve Working of Large Programs through Lean

If you asked people for the definition of lean management, you will often get different answers. Experts have stated that organizations with lean management have better experience, systems and higher profitability.

It is true that customer satisfaction is the primary focus in lean thinking and the idea is to remove any activities that a customer is not willing to pay for.

If people looked beyond these goals, they will observe that lean is quite complex and comprises of multiple elements. The following notions of lean have been identified:

- Lean management as a fixed goal or state which can loosely be translated into being lean
- Lean management as a defined set of working methods
- Lean management as a process of continuous improvement
- Lean management as an application philosophy

The key for any business willing to apply lean thinking is to identify a plan and start. It is not an easy task to transform a business into a lean business overnight and the process to become lean does not end.

Most businesses make the mistake of trying to become perfect as soon as they can. They forget that they must first improve their processes and become better before they can achieve perfection.

This chapter covers some ideas to help you implement lean management in the organization.

Work in Process related teams

Instead of working in financial roles or teams, process operators must work with teams that are process oriented. In most businesses and processes, the management is notified of any problem that may have arisen in the process and the management identifies a person who can solve that problem.

However, it is better to have teams that are self-directed, in the sense that there are people to address problems and solve them. A business can start with the necessary tools, but it should also understand that both thought and management must be changed for the organization to become a lean business.

Often businesses do not transform into lean businesses not because of the failure to understand how lean tools and techniques need to be used, but the failure to change the management.

Correctly coach staff

If a business selects a few people to coach on how lean thinking can be implemented to improve processes, it will create a management group that can work with different teams and facilitate change and removes waste from the process.

The staff must first do and then be trained. It is unfortunate that staff cannot be trained to think or learn lean through PowerPoint. The principle of lean or the Toyota way is always to learn by doing.

There are different approaches to applying lean thinking in business.

The Oliver Wight Approach runs an event that is action based which educates the team and also helps the team understand how lean thinking can be embedded into their process.

The team must create a process map and also identify steps that may be waste contributors. Additionally, they are also asked to create a plan and a budget using lean thinking. Another common approach is the Toyota approach where some members of a team are put into difficult situations that they must overcome. They are expected to identify a solution to the problem.

Start with Value Stream Models

As mentioned earlier, value stream mapping is a key principle of lean thinking. If this tool is used correctly, then the business can create a map of the process that is of value to the business and those that are waste contributors.

The value stream map is then used to understand why certain processes are considered waste and how they can be removed. Value stream mapping is a tool that should only be applied to product families that can be transformed immediately.

Implement Kaizen

The trainer or facilitator must be well versed with lean philosophy and tools.

He or she should ensure that the training is focused on one problem since that helps to keep the training relevant to the business and also ensures that there are tangible outcomes from the training.

Through Kaizen, some business processes can be completed in smaller time periods.

Organize around the value stream

In many businesses, management is organized by function or process. Managers own only some steps in the process, but there is nobody who is responsible for the complete value stream. It is recommended that every organization create a matrix where there are heads of departments, but there are managers who are associated with enhancing the value stream.

A person who has excellent leadership skills and is aware of the product and the processes followed should take care of the value stream and be accountable to stakeholders and customers.

Develop Feedback and Communication Channels

Through communication channels, people at different levels and in different teams can share their ideas and build synergy, which will help the business move towards a profitable future.

Feedback channels allow customers to share their views about products and services, which enables the business to improve.

Use Value Stream Metrics

You must eliminate non-lean metrics that wreak havoc within teams and use those metrics that adhere to the value stream. This change will ensure that every employee in the organization works to the best of his or her abilities and delivers products and services of high quality.

Create a Positive Atmosphere

Most businesses will make mistakes when they switch to lean thinking and management. It is crucial to accept those mistakes and learn from them.

The managers and staff in the business must be patient with the progress being made. This helps to create an environment that is blame-free and supportive.

A business should take risks at some stages to push their resources to achieve their goals.

Collect and collate data

Every business is driven by the analyses conducted on different types of data that are collected by various departments in the business. The business must use this data to change processes.

This helps to remove the bias, both professional and emotional, out of decision-making and ensures that every employee in the business accepts the changes made.

It is also good to track the performance of every team and store that data for future reference. It is crucial to remember that lean management is not a project but is a way of business. You must track every process and review the flow regularly to remove any waste contributors.

Set a benchmark

It is always good to learn from businesses that have implemented lean thinking to understand and gain an idea of how it can be implemented in your business.

Most companies are willing to present their change from being a non-lean company to a lean company. Every member in the management should network with the management from other businesses to understand how lean thinking and management can be implemented in their organization.

Never Give Up

It is difficult to change from a non-lean business to a lean business since most staff members are unable to accept change. Over time, they realize that lean thinking improves the processes that are performed in their business.

They learn that they can optimize processes and remove useless or redundant processes from the flow that most customers are unwilling to pay for.

As a business, you must strive to transform both your management and your processes. Remember never to give up since the aim is to build a business that constantly improves to enhance profitability.

Chapter Four: How to Harness Lean to Foster Innovation and Develop New Ideas

There is a lot of talk about innovation and how companies have started to innovate their processes to work efficiently. But, what is the impact of using lean to foster innovation in business? The potential is huge, and it is essential that every business harness that potential if some criteria are met.

The word innovation can either excite or terrify us. Many people are skeptical about the innovation of processes in their company. But, there are others who are embracing this innovation with open arms.

The former group is stuck in their old ways while the latter are willing to unlock their creative potential to improve the business. However, there is one thing that is certain – the leaner a business, the easier it is to innovate the business.

The debate on how lean thinking can foster innovation is one that has gained popularity. But, what is innovation? Innovation can be defined as the process of changing or transforming a process or an idea into something new, which will make the lives of the employees in the business more accessible.

Regardless of what process the business is transforming – manufacturing technology, products, services, software and business models – any innovation should always lead to the maximization and creation of value for the stakeholder or customer.

This means that the business should meet not only the needs and demands of the customer but also anticipate them. Apple is one company that has understood its customer group very well.

I am sure you know where this is leading. Lean is one process that is customer-driven, and every principle and tool is based on the idea of freeing up the business's resources by removing waste and also maximizing the customers' value.

This helps to include newer projects and also allocate some resources to those processes. Many people believe that a lean business can innovate processes since it encourages the employees to identify innovative ways to improve its processes.

The business community has realized that lean thinking is one model that should be used to foster innovation in business. Many organizations have used lean thinking as a foundation to innovate their ideas and processes.

Take Pixar, for instance, which is a company that has implemented feedback loops and team-based collaboration. This has helped employees overcome their creative block thereby triggering innovation.

It is also important to remember that it is not only businesses that can benefit from lean thinking. Social, economic and environmental problems have become driving forces behind innovation. People and businesses should be respectful and mindful of the resources of our planet before they begin to innovate.

This innovation should contribute to solving the challenges of our time. Toyota Automotive has taught the world that lean thinking improves the society. This is further proof that lean thinking and innovation are a perfect match.

It has been proved that lean thinking is more superior to traditional manufacturing. But, one has to remember that lean thinking is more about improving the management system and leadership behavior.

Lean drives innovation and is an approach that is based on learning. However, certain conditions have to be in place for lean management to succeed.

Organizational Structure for Lean Innovation

An organization must have the right structure to foster innovation through lean thinking. Companies must always be inclusive in the sense that every stakeholder must participate in the decisions that the company makes.

For example, employees, engineers, suppliers, scientists and customers must agree upon every decision that is made by the company to maximize value for the customers. Every function that takes place in a business must be included in innovation, and this is what lean thinking teaches us.

The phenomenon of "open innovation" arises when every team in an organization is included in the process of innovation. This concept suggests that every innovative idea must be welcome even if it is coming from outside the organization. Businesses can take ideas that were coined by college students, scientists, young entrepreneurs and sometimes amateurs as well.

A striking example of this phenomenon is Wikipedia. Any person who has additional information about a particular concept can make changes to pages in Wikipedia. Some traditional organizations are catching up and accepting products that were invented outside the organization.

A company that is open to innovation must have a flat organizational structure since vertical structures have been known to fail. Business leaders must always identify the processes or layers in the structure that add value to their customers.

There are a few strategies that a business can use to foster innovation through lean thinking in their organization.

How to Start the Process of Innovation and Experimentation

Understand why

Most businesses have started to innovate their processes. As mentioned earlier, the ideas can be taken from outside the business. This does not mean that a business should always choose ideas from outside the organization. If the business is unable to sketch or draft an idea that can maximize value for the customers, it does not understand the process fully. Additionally, it cannot implement new ideas successfully if it does not understand how those ideas benefit the company and the customer.

Business Factors

The management must always look at the business factors in their business and their competitors' businesses. If the factors used to conduct processes are the same, no innovation has been made to the process. This reduces the competitive advantage that the business may have over its competitors.

Business Model Diagram

If there are any competitive barriers, they must be removed to start improving and innovating processes. The management must outline the key activities, partners, cost structure, revenue stream and value propositions and observe them keenly to understand if any changes can be made.

Value Matrix

If there are any products or services that the customers do not appreciate or want, these can be removed from the value stream to enhance the process. This allows businesses to invest in fewer resources and add more value to the products and services. Businesses will have the ability to elevate the elements of the business that are bringing in more value and also create different purchases that are in line with the demands of the customers.

Strategy Profile

Businesses must revisit their business strategies and their competitors to identify areas where they can innovate and newer areas of business that can be tapped into. This will help the business identify new areas of work and also develop products and services within that area of work.

Business Model Diagram

Businesses must always identify ways to solve problems and also identify new ways to develop and enhance customer relationships. There was one landscaping company that passed the following message to different households by flinging Frisbees into their yards – "We work on your neighbor's lawn. Let us work on yours too!"

If the customer had never thought of hiring a landscaping company before, they might think about it twice since it will make their life easier.

Experimentation

Every business is allowed to fail. If there is a new concept that has been developed, the business should put it into action to see how the customers view it. There is a possibility that the idea may fail, but it is all right to fail. This helps the business identify what can be done better the next time an idea is implemented.

Renewal

Ideas that have been implemented should never be ignored. The business must revisit the ideas and see what can be improved to enhance customer experience. Always make upgrades to existing ideas since innovation is an ongoing process.

Chapter Five: How to Foster Learning and Experimentation through Lean

A learning organization is not different from lean management. Learning is a process that is embedded in lean management. An organization where teams learn from everyday processes and also experiment with innovations and changes made to a process is called a lean and learning organization.

Every employee in an organization must learn every day about the processes and enhance their knowledge of the processes. This will enable the employees to cater to any problems that may occur during the process. Every employee must focus on the following questions:

- What have I learned today?
- Have I implemented any new changes to an existing process?
- Have I experimented with new processes?
- What is the data trying to tell me today?

Learning organizations are not the current trend, and there are very few businesses that have begun to learn about the processes and have tried to innovate those processes.

What every business must remember is that learning provides the business with an environment where employees are given the freedom to think and also embrace the idea that solutions to work-related problems are found in their mind.

The employee must always tap into his or her knowledge base and use that knowledge to develop concepts and ideas that will improve the process.

In a lean business, learning is not restricted to training only. Training does help the employees develop some skills and also grasp and understanding of how the company functions. But, through learning, the employees will develop better skills and more knowledge that can enhance the profitability of the company.

Learning Model

The following learning model can be implemented in businesses to enhance learning.

Level 1

Every employee must learn the process, procedures, understand why a process is being done the way it is and also some essential facts about the process. This is a level of learning that applies to processes where only minor changes can be made.

Level 2

Learn new skills that can be transferred to situations at work. If the employee is in a new situation or has been shifted to a new process, he or she must have the ability to respond to changes in the process. The business can also choose to bring in outside expertise for this level of learning. There can be training that will help employees enhance their skills.

Level 3

Employees must always learn to adapt. This is a level of learning that applies to situations that are dynamic and where every solution must be developed. Experimentation and learning from failure are two ways of learning in this level.

Level 4

This is where an employee learns to learn. This is about how an employee can be creative and innovate processes. He or she can learn to design processes for the future. Knowledge is reframed at this level, and every assumption made by an employee is challenged.

Learning organizations set employees free. They are not required to be passive players in the business but can learn to express their views and ideas and also challenge those ideas and their skills to improve the work environment. Employees can create an environment where they can create and achieve the results that they truly desire.

Learning Culture

It is difficult to establish a learning culture in organizations that are not lean since they are comfortable in old practices and rarely find the necessity to change their processes. That being said, it is hard to establish a learning culture in any business. This section provides some aspects that a business should consider when it is keen on developing a learning culture.

External or Future Orientation

Organizations that have external or future orientation can understand their environment. Some teams comprise of senior members of the organization who take some time out of their busy day to develop a plan for the future. Additionally, the business can also choose to employ advisors who can help them plan their business.

Free Flow and Exchange of Information

There should be some systems in place that ensure that there are experts available whenever needed. Employees must have the chance to expand their horizons and also network with employees or professionals from other companies. This will give them an opportunity to enhance their knowledge of different processes, which will help them become experts in the process.

Commitment to Personal Development and Learning

With the support from the top management, employees must have the chance to learn. Employees who make an effort to learn regularly must be rewarded. This act will ensure that other employees also step forward and learn more. The employees must also be given the time to learn and also be encouraged to think lean which will help to remove waste from processes.

Trust and Openness

Every individual must be encouraged to develop or create ideas that will improve processes. They must also be allowed to voice their opinion, even if it is different from what other employees think since that gives rise to diversity. Views should be challenged.

Valuing Employees

Any idea that is developed by an employee should be tried and tested. An employee must be valued, and his or her thought process must be stimulated. If the idea is experimented and fails, the employee must learn from that failure and develop an idea that overcomes any errors.

In simpler words, a learning organization does not only implement ideas developed by senior management. It also allows employees to express their views.

Lean thinking is about creating a learning organization

It is important to remember that lean businesses are not only about the processes, it is also about learning. Every process is a great tool to transform an organization into a learning organization.

This should be the goal that every organization must achieve in the current market and economy. The disruption, complexity and change are going to continue, and the rate at which these phenomena are occurring will only increase with time.

The only competitive advantage that any business has in this economy is the ability to adapt, and the only way a business can adapt is by learning continually.

If a business wants to compete in the information-saturated economy, it is necessary for it to remain competitive, dynamic and to look for ways to improve its processes.

It is essential to remember that change is the only constant in every organization and every business must rid itself of the traditional hierarchy that often averse to change.

A learning organization embraces change and creates reference points that help to rebuild the structure. Learning organizations are healthier since they:

- Increase the ability to accept and manage change
- Garner and encourage independent thought
- Improve quality
- Give employees hope that things can always get better

- Develop a committed organization and workforce
- Stretch and expand perceived limits

To create a learning organization the management or leadership must be effective. This means that leadership cannot follow the traditional hierarchy but must consist of a mixed group of people from different levels in the system.

The business must also accept that every employee can solve some problems that may occur in the organization. The business must give employees the benefit of doubt and encourage them to voice their opinion, which will help the business forge ahead and create a bright future.

An organization must never consider itself separate from the world. It is only when it connects to the world that it can build a learning culture and environment.

One of the biggest challenges that every business must overcome is the way it identifies people within the organization.

Only when every employee is considered equal is there a possibility to develop a learning organization.

Chapter Six: How can a Business Identify Value with Lean

Lean businesses always identify ways to maximize the value for their customers, which is the core objective of lean thinking. Most people are under the notion that lean thinking can only be implemented in sales and marketing departments since those departments work directly with customers.

This is not true since lean thinking is now being used to deliver value products to stakeholders of all departments.

Most people view lean as a tool that can be used to eliminate waste from processes and internal mechanisms thereby maximizing the value for the customer. But lean is a business process and kaizen is its cultural center.

This is an important aspect to consider when a business wants to identify the value of long-term processes. Most businesses still believe that lean thinking is a way for the demand side since they are not looking at the value stream.

These businesses can make better profits since the demand for their products exceeds their supply.

However, most businesses are in a market where supply exceeds demand. Take mobile phones for instance. Numerous companies have been set up in different parts of the world that develop new phone models every day.

However, most people choose to purchase Apple products, because the business has catered to the demands of the product and has always tried to identify ways to maximize the value of the customer. Therefore, businesses must remember that lean is not only about removing waste from the process, but also about identifying ways to enhance the value stream to maximize the value of the product.

There is no company in today's economy that rejects more prospects or refuses orders. The business must always look for ways to drive revenue.

Therefore, a business must improve continually to enhance and improve the processes in the value stream. So, how does a business use lean thinking to identify value?

- Understand the demands of stakeholders and customers
- Identify elements in the process that are waste contributors and those that affect the quality of the product

If a business is implementing lean thinking, it must eliminate processes that contribute to waste and those that do not add any value to the product or service. A business will view every activity that it performs and views the steps to see if each of them adds value to the final product or service.

An activity is defined as a waste contributor if it adds cost and takes time to complete but does not improve the final product that is delivered to the stakeholder or customer. Every business focuses on how to shorten the timeline and how the value flow between the business and customer can be improved.

The value is identified by becoming a faster, cheaper and better business. In simpler words, a business must always change its processes to produce goods and services that a customer is willing to pay for.

Another way to identify value is by defining the internal customers or stakeholders. These internal stakeholders are members of each department that use outputs of one department as input to achieve their business goals and objectives.

Regardless of whether a business is working with internal or external customers, it must focus on how the customers are satisfied rather how well they are satisfied. The fundamental of lean thinking then changes to the following – "if a process is improved, the value of the process is also improved."

Most businesses are product-focused. These businesses cannot view the market or access the market to become the best. They also make the mistake of looking at the value of the product or service and how it will help the customer.

Businesses must remember that the idea of value is abstract and there is no real definition. The business must always identify ways to create, identify and deliver value to its customers.

Ways to Add Value

Faster and Better

The business must identify ways to deliver products of high quality to customers either before the promised time or on time. Every individual is impatient and a person who has finally taken a look at a product will want it yesterday. If the business can deliver faster, more customers will flock towards the business since there is a direct perceived correlation between the value of offering and the speed at which it is offered.

Better Quality

The key is to remember that every customer wants products that are of better quality. Therefore, every business must develop products that are of greater quality when compared to the products of its competitors. A business must remember that the customer defines quality. A business must always find out what its customers want and develop products with high quality for them.

Always Add More Value

Always add value to the product. Most businesses in an industry deliver the same or similar products. For any business to stand out, it must offer something that other businesses do not offer. Apple is an excellent example of this point.

Increase convenience

You have to identify ways to eliminate processes that make it difficult for customers to place their orders with ease. There are issues when the customer needs to go through elaborate processes to place an order. If that is the case, customers will choose businesses where it is easy for them to place their orders. Lean thinking plays a key role here since the business will need to identify waste contributors and remove them thereby adding value to the process.

Improve Customer Service

It is important to remember that human beings are emotional and this is a factor that every business must include in its customer service. The business must identify a way to tap into the emotions of its customers by being warm, friendly, cheerful and helpful. A business must ensure that it always helps its customers regardless of how big or small the request is.

Changing Lifestyle

Businesses must identify how lifestyles are changing and how these changes impact customers. They must collect data and make sound decisions to improve the value of their products and services. It is important to understand that every customer has a different taste and a business must find a way to tap into those tastes and deliver products of excellent quality.

A business can also have the ability to move into new markets and provide customers with better products and services.

Offer Discounts

Planned discounting will add value and wealth to a business. If a business has a surplus of products, it must identify ways to sell those products in higher volumes. Most supermarkets, like Costco, give customers the chance to buy large volumes of a product at a lower rate.

The business can also pass on the savings to the customer and also make profits by selling more significant volumes of some products.

When a business wants to identify ways to enhance the value of its products and services, it will look at ways to increase the speed at which it delivers products and also find ways to improve the quality of the products.

This is when they begin to innovate and identify new processes that can maximize the value of a product for the customer. Businesses must always function with the customers in their minds since they define the business.

If a customer believes that a business is honest and the products delivered are of great quality, word will spread across the market and more customers will switch to that business.

Therefore, a business must always identify ways to enhance value for its customers.

Conclusion

Lean thinking is a way of business and not just a business project. There are only some businesses that have begun to use lean thinking to enhance and improve processes and also maximize customer value.

The group of businesses that do not implement lean thinking is afraid of change. However, change is the only constant in the market and life.

Lean thinking requires a change not only in the processes but also in the management and leadership since the business has to be open to new thoughts and ideas.

Through lean management and thinking, a business can encourage its employees to identify ways to improve processes and also innovate or develop new processes that maximize value.

This creates a sense of equality in the organization since every employee has the right to voice his or her opinion.

Over the course of the book, you will learn about lean thinking and the different principles and tools of lean thinking. The book will also help you understand how an environment for innovation and learning can be built in the business.

A business must always work towards maximizing value. This book covers some points that a business must consider to do the same.

Thank you for purchasing this book. I hope you have gathered all the necessary information.

www.ingramcontent.com/pod-product-compliance
Lightning Source LLC
Chambersburg PA
CBHW071157220526
45468CB00003B/1058